This page is intentionally left blank.

Copyright

Intro

I want to start by giving you a background on solo ads. Here's how I define solo ads for the purpose of this training: a solo ad is an email advertisement that you will purchase from someone else in your niche that has an email list. That person will send your email advertisement out to their list recommending that their subscribers take a look at your ad. That's my formal definition of solo ads.

When you think about purchasing a solo ad, you're purchasing an email that's going to be sent out to somebody who is in your niche that has subscribers on their list who meet your target market. In that email there is going to be either a link to an opt-in page so that people can become subscribers on your list, or, there will be a link to a sales page if you prefer to build your list with buyers instead of subscribers.

I'm going to teach you how to find people in your niche from whom to purchase solo ads. I'll also give you some of the details for how you can continually grow your list over time through the use of these solo ads.

When to Avoid Commercial Solo Ad Providers

Before I get into the core techniques, I want to warn you to be careful with commercial solo ad providers: What I'm going to teach you is how to find people whose list you can mail, so you can purchase solo ads from individuals who are in the business of building a quality niche list just like you are. I want to contrast that against a commercial solo ad provider.

What is a commercial solo ad provider?

That is generally someone who has created a list for the express purpose of selling you a mailing to their list. What happens here is, if someone is in the business only of getting as many clicks as possible to your email advertisement (so that you will purchase that solo ad from that individual) their goal is to find as many subscribers as possible who like to click ads. That's their goal – at least, that's their secondary goal.

Their first goal is to sell as many solo ads as possible.

Somehow they need to get folks on their list, so thy're perhaps going to buy a solo ad to somebody else's list so that they can get say 10k subscribers on their list. Maybe they buy 100 solo ads, get 100 subscribers from each solo add, and now they have a list of 10k solo ad subscribers. Then they sell 2 solo ads a day morning and night and send this list of 10k your ad in the morning, somebody else's in the afternoon, somebody else's the next morning, somebody else's in the afternoon.

What happens to the quality of this list? It just goes down, and down, and down, and down.

As a result of this, if you buy solo ads from those types of commercial solo ad providers you're not going to get the kind of results that you can get from solo ads. I think that this is where some of the confusion has come in with solo ads.

When we have a discussion about solo ads, and I say "Hey, I ran a solo ad, and did really well with it," then next week, I say phrase "Be really careful with solo ads," there's a real disconnect there!

The problem is, I'm using the word solo ad to

possible.

Somehow they need to get folks on their list, so thy're perhaps going to buy a solo ad to somebody else's list so that they can get say 10k subscribers on their list. Maybe they buy 100 solo ads, get 100 subscribers from each solo add, and now they have a list of 10k solo ad subscribers. Then they sell 2 solo ads a day morning and night and send this list of 10k your ad in the morning, somebody else's in the afternoon, somebody else's the next morning, somebody else's in the afternoon.

What happens to the quality of this list? It just goes down, and down, and down, and down.

As a result of this, if you buy solo ads from those types of commercial solo ad providers you're not going to get the kind of results that you can get from solo ads. I think that this is where some of the confusion has come in with solo ads.

When we have a discussion about solo ads, and I say "Hey, I ran a solo ad, and did really well with it," then next week, I say phrase "Be really careful with solo ads," there's a real disconnect there!

The problem is, I'm using the word solo ad to describe two different things. They're both solo ads, and that's why I'm using that word to describe both things. In one case, I'm using the word solo ad to describe what originally was a solo ad – an email ad drop with a reputable niche list. That is where you contact an individual and you say "hey, can I mail to your list, and what's it going to cost me?"

Now, because of all these commercial solo ad providers, you might be thinking when you hear solo ad provider: "okay, let me go to this list of 25 people who sell solo ads, because I bought the list somewhere and it's a great list and everybody's really excited about it, I'm just going to go buy a bunch of solo ads and build a list."

Because you heard me say in one breath "I bought a solo ad and it converted, I've used solo ads to generate traffic." Maybe you didn't hear me say "You don't want to buy those commercial solo ads." I just want to be really clear here that you're going to go out and you're going to find solo ads to lists who are not mailed a whole lot of solo ads. Instead, the list has been built for the purpose of monetizing it in-house.

When you mail a solo ad to a list that's been built in-house, it's going to be mailed to a strong list. Just like if you mailed to my list, or you've mailed to your list. You're building a strong quality list of people who really trust you.

Let's just say someone did come to you and they said "Hey, I've got something I offer that I believe would be valuable to your subscribers. Would you be interested in mailing it to your list (for a fee or a payment, of course)? Let's just say that you say "I might be interested, let me see the offer, how much are you interested in paying?" And the person says "Well, I'll give you $300 for mailing this offer out to your list." You look at it and you think that will really help my list. Yes, I'll take the $300 and you mail it out to your list.

If you only do that once or twice a month, you and your client, the person that bought that solo ad from you, are likely going to get a good response from that mailing. We contrast that from what I just shared with you where somebody's mailing twice a day these 3rd party offers, and conversion just really tends to go down.

Now, having said all of that, you CAN try out and test solo ad providers from the commercial sources . . . just be sure and test each one individually for not only new subscribers, but for sales.

Commercial solo ad sellers can be an easy way

to get fast leads, but if you spend $1000 and get 1000 leads who never ever buy . . .then it's not a good investment.

All of that said . . test and try solo ad providers, but recognize the possible pitfalls.

Two sources of solo ad providers: http://udimi.com/

That's a POWERFUL solo ad source . .

or you can purchase one of these solo ad "trainings" or rolodexes that give additional commercial solo ad training or lists of solo ad providers (note to plr buyer, these are my affiliate links, replace with yours at http://warriorplus.com), and you can choose to only feature one or two of these, your choice . .

https://warriorplus.com/o2/a/z2yn3/0
https://warriorplus.com/w/a/zskyg
https://warriorplus.com/o2/a/zjtby/0
https://warriorplus.com/o2/a/hwc6z/0

How Do You Find Solo Ads in Your Niche?

You're going to find other people who have lists, and then you're going to go out and ask them if you can buy a mailing to their lists. In a sentence, that's exactly what you're going to do.

I'm going to give you step by step exactly what to do and how to do it:

The very first thing that you're going to do is you are going to build your own private in-house list of other people who have lists in your niche. You may want to open a new email address (so you can use a throwaway email address). Or you can use another email address that's on your server. This is going to be a separate email address.

You're going to join everybody's list in your niche. Now, if you're in a huge niche you may not want to join everybody's list. You want to join 50 or 100 lists in your niche. You're going to get emails from the lists you've joined. Some people may mail once or twice a day. If you join 100 lists on your main email address and everybody sends out 1 email a day, you're going to get an extra 100 emails to your inbox; it's going to be distracting. Set up a new email address ☺

Again, you're going to join everybody's list in

your niche that you can possibly join. I'm going to give you a few creative ways to do that quickly in just a moment.

However, before I give that to you I want to say this: you may find that you're already a member of 3 or 4 lists. You may find that some of the people whose lists you're on send you, from time to time, offers to get on someone else's list. There's an organic process here. In the course of reading your email you can unsubscribe from the main list and resubscribe with email address you're doing this monitoring from. Get them all into that central location. You're going to want them in a central location that you can scroll through them. I'll teach you that in just a moment.

Make an effort to join every list possible when the opportunity arises. In 30 days you may be on 15 or 20 or 25 lists anyhow. You want to make this happen really quickly. There's a few different ways that you can do it:

- Go to your favorite search engine and type in your niche name. Get on any lists you come to.

- You can type 25 different keywords that are related to what you're doing – you don't have to limit it to just one. You just scroll through every single one of those

- listings and look for ways to get on someone's list.

If someone doesn't have a way to get onto their list, you can probably assume that they either don't have a list, or they're not aggressively building one. Maybe they don't care about mailing to their list. They're probably not a great prospect anyhow for what we're talking about here.

So you should not go out of your way to find a way to get on someone's list. If they're not advertising "get on my list" or f you go to someone's blog, and there's no opt-in that says "Hey, get a free gift for giving me your name and email address." There's not a pop-up that says "Here's a free gift for getting onto my list, click here." If you're not seeing any of that occur, then don't go out of the way to get onto that person's list. My guess is that they're not actively building or developing that list.

Even if they're mailing, if they're not fresh with their list, this is probably not the kind of list that you want to mail. If someone aggressively built their list 3 years ago, but they're not adding any new subscribers today, the list probably does not have enough people on it who are currently interested in your topic for you to invest anyhow.

Go through the search rankings, look for squeeze pages, look for opt-in forms, and you're just going to sign up for all of them. Every single one that you find. 50, 100, whatever.

Finding Paid Solo Ads From Adwords Listings

The second place that you can go is the pay-per-click ads. In your search engine, the top, or the side the search page, you may find some advertisements that you can click through. Click through them all. Some of those are going to be squeeze pages.

What do we know about those advertisements? These people are serious about building their lists. Why? They're paying $1 per click or $5 per click or $2 a subscriber or whatever the case is; they're paying good money to build their list right now.

That tells us two things:

- #1, they're aggressive about building their list.

- #2, and this is really good for you, what we usually know about people who that are paying money to build a list is that they're not fully monetizing those leads right away.

If it takes someone 45 days to break even on their leads, but they're paying a search engine provider $100 / day for those leads, there's a cash flow disconnect. If you go to that individual, you can make an offer that you will pay $2 / subscriber they bring to you. All they have to do is: as soon as somebody joins the list, send them your squeeze page, or even have your squeeze page on their immediate download page, and you'll pay them $2 / subscriber.

Let me show you want that looks like:

Let's say that Johnny is advertising over on one of the search engines. Johnny is paying $1 per click, and he's getting a 33% conversion rate. So 1 out of 3 people becomes a subscriber. 1 out of 3 people becomes a subscriber and he's paying $1 per click, he's paying $3 / subscriber. He's probably not monetizing that right away.

Of course, there's one way for you to find out: you go ahead and sign up for the list. Is there a good one-time offer there? Is there an up-sell?

When you get on his list is there an aggressive offer to get you to invest in something in the first day or two?

Maybe you look at the offer and you think, "I don't know how he's breaking even on this." It's costing him $300 for 100 subscribers, I don't see how he's making $300 here. We probably know that this individual will allow you to immediately mail his list, put it into his email campaign, or even put your opt-in box on his download page. If he's paying $3 / subscriber.

If perhaps 50% of those subscribers were to become your subscribers as well, and you were to pay him $2 apiece, he's going to immediately get a return of $1 per subscriber on his leads. He's getting $2 for the ones that you buy, and you're only buying half of them, because only half of them opt-in to you. His lead cost goes from $3 to $2 immediately because you're doing this. Some people like to monetize their leads right away; they may have 3 offers just like that... and you're one of those offers.

This is a unique situation with people that are buying leads, and we know that they're buying leads, so that's a tactic you can try if you see an ad campaign that seems successful.

Mining Email Lists for Opportunity

Now you've gotten on 50 people's lists. You're going to get an email every day, or every other day, from these 50 people in this specialized email account.

What you're going to do is: for the 1st 30 days you're going to open every email that you get in that email account.

Please let me say this, if you're opening 50 emails a day, you MUST become methodical about it and only spend 20 seconds on each email. All you want to do is open the emails, maybe click some of the links in the emails.

Get a feel for what Julie is doing on her list. Is she just spamming everybody all the time? What kind of offers does Julie have? Johnny over here, what kind of list does he have? He's always sending out only high-quality information. You may even want to have a notebook and put Johnny's name, and Julie's name, and Becky's name, and Tom's name, and write down your feelings about the list. Are they good emails? Are they connecting?

Here's the thing, if you mail to a list that you feel good about the emails, you're probably going to get a really good response. Which means that you can pay more for that solo ad.

But, if you don't feel good about the email campaign, if you feel like that person is just sell, sell, sell and there's no relationship building... You probably don't want to mail that person's list at all. Maybe you should even unsubscribe from that list so that it comes out of your collection of potential people to buy from.

In 30 days we're going to go back to this list of 50 email lists to ask them if we can do a solo ad. I'll teach you how to do that in just a moment.

Another Reason to Monitor Mailing Lists

There's another purpose to clicking every one of those emails, every single day. Remember, it should only take you 20 minutes to do the 50 emails. They're in a separate email account, which you're going to open only once day. You're not going to open it every 10 minutes like you might do with your smart phone.

means that you can pay more for that solo ad.

But, if you don't feel good about the email campaign, if you feel like that person is just sell, sell, sell and there's no relationship building... You probably don't want to mail that person's list at all. Maybe you should even unsubscribe from that list so that it comes out of your collection of potential people to buy from.

In 30 days we're going to go back to this list of 50 email lists to ask them if we can do a solo ad. I'll teach you how to do that in just a moment.

Another Reason to Monitor Mailing Lists

There's another purpose to clicking every one of those emails, every single day. Remember, it should only take you 20 minutes to do the 50 emails. They're in a separate email account, which you're going to open only once day. You're not going to open it every 10 minutes like you might do with your smart phone.

This is going to be something you only do once

a day. But every single time that somebody sends you an offer to get on somebody else's list, you're going to take up the offer. After a month you might be on 100 lists instead of 50 lists.

Here's what you'll do after 30 days – and you'll do this by hand. Sometimes people want to automate things. Sometimes it's boring to hand mail 100 emails. I know, I've done it before. Sometimes it's boring. But the return on investment is incredible. If you try to do something sneaky like BCC 100 people, people know it. Do you know it when somebody BCC's you? You do, right? You know it? I know it. They know it. If they see that, it's not a personal email anymore. You think it is, and you're trying to pull off as a personal email, but it's not a personal email, you know it, and they know it.

You're going to do this by hand.

Now, you can hire someone to do this for you, but hire someone you trust. Don't go over to a freelancing website and hire somebody you don't know to do this as their first project for you. If they don't do it right, you've lost all of the goodwill and energy and effort that you've put into this project for the last 30 days.

This is going to take a good bit of time. And

actually, I don't recommend you outsource it. Do it yourself. There's plenty of other routine things that you can do in your business. But getting an intimate gut feeling for the kinds of people who are in your niche that you can build a relationship with and make a lot of money on these relationships - possibly for the rest of your life, but certainly as long as you run your business – that's something you want to do.

This is something that you want to be...

A) set up right, not to say that if you outsource it, it won't be done right. But if you hire somebody brand new you don't know if it will be done right.

B) there is a value in just having a feeling for each one of these people's lists, and you can't buy a feeling. You can't pay Becky $300 to give you a feeling. What you have to do is, you have to go out there and get that feeling yourself.

By taking 20 minutes every single day and just reading everybody's email. That's the only way you'll find out... is Tom a good guy? Is Becky a good gal? Is Mark a good guy? Is Johnny a good guy? Is Steven a good guy? That's the only way that you'll find out.

Sample Email Script

After 30 days you're going to write each person a personalized email. I'm going to give you a sample script here. But, it's just a sample. The reason I stress this is so often when I use the word script, people just copy and paste what I say. But, it doesn't fit your style.

I'm going to give you some words that I might use if I were to pen this email right now:

This email is basically going to tell them "Hey, I have a list in your niche, I think it could be valuable to your subscribers, would you be interested in doing some kind of mailing?" There's a few different ways that you can phrase that, I'll write what I would uses if I were to be emailing someone today. But 30 days from now it might be different. It would be the words that I came up with that day. Today it might look like:

> Dear Johnny,
>
> My name is John Doe, and I've been on your list for about 30 days. I appreciate the value that you give your subscribers. (Or maybe you've learned something

from that list, I appreciate the things that I've learned from you. Or, maybe you've bought something from them. I appreciated learning about X Y Z in your A B C training.) I've got a quick question for you. I'm in kind of a related niche, I teach people how to do X Y Z, and I believe that some of my training might be helpful to some of your subscribers. Would you be open to talking about doing some kind of mailing or solo ad or ad swap, etc. to your list? If so, let me know.

And, you can let them hit reply to the email.

If you would like to use Skype perhaps, say, "hey, here's my Skype handle." Or here's my email address. Or, if you would like to talk to them on the phone, you could include your phone number.

Trust me, you're mailing professional list owners that have real lists. You're not going to get a whole bunch of phone calls from people that are going to waste your time. If they call you, it's going to be a valuable 5-minute phone call. You put your phone number in the email: they call you, or they Skype you, or they email you back. They say "I would like to know a little bit more about what you have, or what your offer is, or what you want to do." If they that I've learned from you. Or, maybe you've bought something from them. I appreciated learning about X Y Z in your A B C training.) I've got a quick question for you. I'm in kind of a related niche, I teach people how to do X Y Z, and I believe that some of my training might be helpful to some of your subscribers. Would you be open to talking about doing some kind of mailing or solo ad or ad swap, etc. to your list? If so, let me know.

And, you can let them hit reply to the email.

If you would like to use Skype perhaps, say, "hey, here's my Skype handle." Or here's my email address. Or, if you would like to talk to them on the phone, you could include your phone number.

Trust me, you're mailing professional list owners that have real lists. You're not going to get a whole bunch of phone calls from people that are going to waste your time. If they call you, it's going to be a valuable 5-minute phone call. You put your phone number in the email: they call you, or they Skype you, or they email you back. They say "I would like to know a little bit more about what you have, or what your offer is, or what you want to do." If they don't look at the offer, that's a red flag right there, they SHOULD look at the offer.

Talking with the List Owner

Then you talk about what you want to do. In this discussion (and this can be done via email, Skype, telephone, whatever) you're going to find out a few things. How many subscribers do they have? If someone has 7 subscribers, you probably don't want to mail their list. Here's a sample conversation:

"How many subscribers do you have?"

"Well, I have 1700 subscribers. I have 7k subscribers."

"How many clicks or opens do you normally get?"

Now, when I've taught this in the past, people sometimes ask me, "well, what's a good open rate and good click-through rate?" It doesn't matter. It's not relevant, I don't care. Somebody could have a 2% click through rate and I could make a lot of money on that mailing. Somebody else could have a 30% click-through rate, but the people on their list are not buyers. I won't make any money at all.

For me to give you a click-through rate, or an open rate as a guideline would just lead you astray. I'm not going to give you one. There isn't one.

You're just going to listen to what's happening for the person you're talking to is saying: if the person says, "well, normally I get 4 clicks per email," that's probably not somebody you want to mail to.

If they say, "I get 50 or 100 clicks per mailing," that's more what you want to mail to if you're just getting started.

If somebody says I get 2k clicks per mailing, that may be somebody you want to mail to, but if it's your very first solo ad, you probably don't. Here's why:

A 2k click solo ad is going to be much more expensive than a 50 click solo ad. And if you've never done a solo ad, you have absolutely no idea if your offer is going to convert when you send it out. So you really need to get some 50 or 100 or 200 clicks under your belt just to find out if your offer converts. If you've just written a squeeze page, and you're not experienced in the business, you have absolutely no idea if it's going to convert.

If the 2000-click list owner happens to be the first person you talk to, you could suggest "Well, let's just mail a portion of your list, and see how the offer does." Tell the truth: "It's a brand new offer, I'm not sure how well it will convert, why don't we just mail 10% of your list and see what happens, if it goes well, hey, we'll ramp up and mail the whole thing, or we'll mail 50% of it, or whatever the case is."

Determining How Much to Pay

Then you're going to have to agree on a price. That's another question I get "What's a fair price?" I'm not going to give you an exact price here. I hesitate to name anything at all, but I know you want something.

Let me try and explain: I want you to get the picture that it's okay to pay $20 / subscriber if you have a back end in place and those are good subscribers and you end up making $200 a piece on them. It's okay to pay $20 / subscriber.

On the other hand, it's not okay to pay 10¢ for a subscriber if all you're going to be able to do is turn that 10¢ subscriber into 20¢ in revenue.

The number that you're going to pay per click or per subscriber should be dictated based on your potential revenue from whatever it is you're doing.

For example, if you are able to generate $20 per subscriber over the course of the year, you might be willing to pay $2 or $3 per subscriber up front to build your list.

What if you're just starting out, and you have no idea about your back end? You don't even have a product, you're just trying to get 500 subscribers on your list so that you can send them some emails and find out what kind of product you should make...

Maybe you pay $2 / subscriber, so it'll cost you $1k to get 500 subscribers, and you're not going to make any money on these individuals right away. You're going to have to create your product. It might take you 2 weeks to create your product the way that I teach to create a product. So you'll get a percentage of those people to buy, and maybe you'll break even on your ad. But you're not going to have anything to sell them the first 2 weeks.

When you build that first part of the list, you simply have to look at it as an investment. Once you've done this 25 times, you should know over time how much you make on average per subscriber. Why don't I give you a quick formula?

Let's just say that you get 1k new subscribers every single month. And you generate $20k every single month. You're averaging $20 / subscriber.

Another way to look at this would be to look at an actual basket of subscribers. Let's say you get 1k subscribers. Then you track THOSE 1k subscribers separately from everybody else for a year, and those 1k subscribers generate $20k. That's another way to do it.

I find that just using the monthly new subscribers, divided into the total number of revenue that you have, gives you a nice average.

Now, if one month you generate 100 subscribers because you don't do much of anything, and the next month you spend $5k and get 2k subscribers, and the next month you only get 100 subscribers, then you have to take a rolling average of the number of subscribers each month and divide that into a rolling average of your revenue because your revenue is going to be driven by the number of new subscribers, but it's not going to correlate month to month. The reason for this is because people don't make all of their expenditures the first month they get on your list. I think that's enough depth on that.

It's just a quick process: how many subscribers are you getting, how much money are you making, that's your $/subscriber. Once you know that, then you can think about how much can I pay per subscriber.

Normally when you buy your solo ad, you can negotiate to pay per subscriber. Paying per click is more common. Obviously, per click becomes a little bit tricky, because you don't know what your subscriber cost is going to be, especially for the first few solo ads that you run. Let's just imagine that you have an opt-in page that has a 25% conversion rate. You want to be at $2 / subscriber. Then you're going to have to get 4 visitors, or 4 clicks, to get one subscriber. So you're going to want to pay 50¢/click to get to $2 / subscriber.

You may be talking with someone they'll only sell you something that's $1/click. You have to ask yourself, is this list going to be strong enough that I can monetize $4 / subscriber? Again, if it's your first list, set $1k aside and just use that as your seed money, as your investment money, to build that first list of 500 or 1k individuals.

Your pricing is just going to be a negotiation.

Ad Swaps

When I gave the sample letter above, I asked if the list owner was interested in doing some kind of mailing – perhaps a solo ad or an ad swap.

Let's talk about what an ad swap is.

An ad swap is a solo ad where you give them a reciprocating solo ad. Instead of paying Johnny $300 to mail your ad to his list, and then having him pay you $300 to mail his ad to your list, you just do a swap. He mails your list, and you mail his list.

Those are the steps to driving traffic with solo ads and finding your own solo ad providers.

Buying Ad Drops to Very Large Lists

There are two more things I want to share with you to wrap up this training.

From time to time you'll come across some big emailers in your niche. Maybe somebody that has a 150k subscribers. And they don't go by "Johnny" anymore. They go by the such-and-such mailing corporation. At first glance you might look at that and think they're commercial and not a good fit for you.

But, if they're not in the business of selling as many solo ads as possible, they may be a good choice. Maybe they advertise that five times a month they open up a solo ad spot. That may be an email that you could be interested in sending.

With those types of relationships, you basically buy your way in. They're saying we do five mailings a month, and to mail to our list it's $2k a mailing. This is what it is. Because it's a huge, mass list, you're probably not going to get the same conversion rate response as you would on a smaller list.

As you grow your business... let's say you're running something new, and you want to get 5k subscribers next month, well that's a lot of work if you do it 50 subscribers per mailing. But, if you can get two people, or two companies that can get you 2k subscribers each in their mailings, that's 4k subscribers right away. Then 20 little guys to give you 50 apiece, so you've got your 5k.

So sometimes having a big mailer, even if the

"Johnny" anymore. They go by the such-and-such mailing corporation. At first glance you might look at that and think they're commercial and not a good fit for you.

But, if they're not in the business of selling as many solo ads as possible, they may be a good choice. Maybe they advertise that five times a month they open up a solo ad spot. That may be an email that you could be interested in sending.

With those types of relationships, you basically buy your way in. They're saying we do five mailings a month, and to mail to our list it's $2k a mailing. This is what it is. Because it's a huge, mass list, you're probably not going to get the same conversion rate response as you would on a smaller list.

As you grow your business... let's say you're running something new, and you want to get 5k subscribers next month, well that's a lot of work if you do it 50 subscribers per mailing. But, if you can get two people, or two companies that can get you 2k subscribers each in their mailings, that's 4k subscribers right away. Then 20 little guys to give you 50 apiece, so you've got your 5k.

So sometimes having a big mailer, even if the quality is a little bit lower, can work well to get

"Johnny" anymore. They go by the such-and-such mailing corporation. At first glance you might look at that and think they're commercial and not a good fit for you.

But, if they're not in the business of selling as many solo ads as possible, they may be a good choice. Maybe they advertise that five times a month they open up a solo ad spot. That may be an email that you could be interested in sending.

With those types of relationships, you basically buy your way in. They're saying we do five mailings a month, and to mail to our list it's $2k a mailing. This is what it is. Because it's a huge, mass list, you're probably not going to get the same conversion rate response as you would on a smaller list.

As you grow your business... let's say you're running something new, and you want to get 5k subscribers next month, well that's a lot of work if you do it 50 subscribers per mailing. But, if you can get two people, or two companies that can get you 2k subscribers each in their mailings, that's 4k subscribers right away. Then 20 little guys to give you 50 apiece, so you've got your 5k.

So sometimes having a big mailer, even if the quality is a little bit lower, can work well to get

"Johnny" anymore. They go by the such-and-such mailing corporation. At first glance you might look at that and think they're commercial and not a good fit for you.

But, if they're not in the business of selling as many solo ads as possible, they may be a good choice. Maybe they advertise that five times a month they open up a solo ad spot. That may be an email that you could be interested in sending.

With those types of relationships, you basically buy your way in. They're saying we do five mailings a month, and to mail to our list it's $2k a mailing. This is what it is. Because it's a huge, mass list, you're probably not going to get the same conversion rate response as you would on a smaller list.

As you grow your business... let's say you're running something new, and you want to get 5k subscribers next month, well that's a lot of work if you do it 50 subscribers per mailing. But, if you can get two people, or two companies that can get you 2k subscribers each in their mailings, that's 4k subscribers right away. Then 20 little guys to give you 50 apiece, so you've got your 5k.

So sometimes having a big mailer, even if the quality is a little bit lower, can work well to get

www.ingramcontent.com/pod-product-compliance
Lightning Source LLC
Chambersburg PA
CBHW071159220526
45468CB00003B/1088